SMOOTH FOX

STERN
Set high and carried gaily.

BACK
Short, straight, and strong.

HINDQUARTERS
Strong and muscular.

THIGHS
Long and powerful.

HOCKS
Well bent, perfectly upright and parallel with each other.

STIFLE
Well curved, not turned in or out.

Title Page: Smooth Fox Terriers owned by Christine Bowker.

Photographers: Beth Studios, Martin Booth, John Flinter, Isabelle Francais, Ann Hearn, Jeanie Studios, Ludwig Studios, Pets By Paulette, Photos Today, S. Ross, Linda Sallee-Hill, and Joyce Smith.

Dedication

This book is dedicated to my four grandchildren, Jill, Jamie, Julia and Jake. When I think of dogs, the image of children playing with their family pet comes to mind, and there is no more heart stirring, or comforting and pleasurable thought than a Smooth with his family playmates.

© by T.F.H. Publications, Inc.

Distributed in the UNITED STATES to the Pet Trade by T.F.H. Publications, Inc., One T.F.H. Plaza, Neptune City, NJ 07753; distributed in the UNITED STATES to the Bookstore and Library Trade by National Book Network, Inc. 4720 Boston Way, Lanham MD 20706; in CANADA to the Pet Trade by H & L Pet Supplies Inc., 27 Kingston Crescent, Kitchener, Ontario N2B 2T6; Rolf C. Hagen Inc., 3225 Sartelon St. Laurent-Montreal Quebec H4R 1E8; in CANADA to the Book Trade by Vanwell Publishing Ltd., 1 Northrup Crescent, St. Catharines, Ontario L2M 6P5 ; in ENGLAND by T.F.H. Publications, PO Box 15, Waterlooville PO7 6BQ; in AUSTRALIA AND THE SOUTH PACIFIC by T.F.H. (Australia), Pty. Ltd., Box 149, Brookvale 2100 N.S.W., Australia; in NEW ZEALAND by Brooklands Aquarium Ltd. 5 McGiven Drive, New Plymouth, RD1 New Zealand; in Japan by T.F.H. Publications, Japan—Jiro Tsuda, 10-12-3 Ohjidai, Sakura, Chiba 285, Japan; in SOUTH AFRICA by Lopis (Pty) Ltd., P.O. Box 39127, Booysens, 2016, Johannesburg, South Africa. Published by T.F.H. Publications, Inc.

MANUFACTURED IN THE
UNITED STATES OF AMERICA
BY T.F.H. PUBLICATIONS, INC.

SMOOTH

FOX

TERRIER

A COMPLETE AND RELIABLE HANDBOOK

by Ann Hearn

RX-101

CONTENTS

CHARACTERISTICS OF THE SMOOTH FOX TERRIER

The life expectancy of a Smooth is quite long—approximately 12 to 14 years, depending on the quality of life you provide for him. Nutritious food, daily clean water, bi-monthly grooming sessions that provide an opportunity to assess the physical health of your dog, and disease-preventive inoculations on a timely basis, are all steps necessary to achieve a healthy and happy pet.

Lest they forget their breeding roots, both Wire and Smooth Fox Terriers enjoy "working"; that is, going to ground in contrived holes made by man, after a critter safely caged at the end of the burrow. There are groups of working terrier people scattered over the US that find great pleasure in maintaining the worth of their dogs.

If you take good care of your Smooth Fox Terrier he will live a full and active life.

7

Smooth Fox Terriers are well suited for just about anything. They will excel in obedience, agility, and community work. Tommy and Paint, owned by Donna Procyson-Hodgson.

The American Kennel Club provides the opportunity to hold obedience classes at sanctioned shows, and our Smooths take to this demanding regimen like ducks to water. The breed is so intelligent that they make wonderful obedience dogs. There are many Companion Dog (CD) Smooths officially registered and recognized.

One of the latest advents endorsed by the AKC are the agility trials. This is a grueling but immensely exciting sport. One can sit for hours watching the dogs run up ramps, pause, then run in and out of fake tunnels and more—all on command and timed. Training is intense to prepare for this competition, but the Smooths are wildly passionate about it—as are their owners. There is more to this breed than a pretty face!

Many Smooths across the US participate in programs of great community worth. They go to children's hospitals, senior citizens facilities, and other types of cooperative projects. As ambassadors for all breeds of dog, as well as the Fox Terrier, they bring joy and a smile to some otherwise rather grim circumstances. The Smooth instinctually knows that this is the time to be a best friend. Many Smooths, through official rescue programs, have been placed in the care of someone with a history of deep depression who has literally given up on life. Having the responsibility of caring for a dog, and receiving the overwhelming love given back by a Smooth, has helped many people back on the road to wellness.

There are stars in every breed, and the Smooth is no exception as he takes to the camera and attention like a pro. One frequently sees a Smooth in magazine ads, television and movies. One such hero is Sparky, a Smooth Fox Terrier who enjoys Frisbees and modeling so much he has made a living at it! For several years he has been among the top 30 small Frisbee-catching dogs in the southern region. Dave Huffine, Sparky's owner, tells me that one day while cleaning out the garage, he threw a Frisbee on a whim. Sparky caught it and returned it to his owner with that pleading look of *do it again!* Sparky got better and better as he jumped in the air, twisted his body, and with ears flying, caught the Frisbee and then sailed over Dave's back. As a Smooth is a "go-to-ground" breed, teaching Sparky to become airborne took special training techniques, but proves the intelligence and cooperative spirit of this breed. In 1995, Sparky was Highest Scoring Freestyle Small Dog Frisbee Champion in the country. Pretty neat stuff for an earth dog!

Once the Freestyle Small Dog Frisbee Champion, Sparky, seen here with owner Dave Huffine, is the perfect example of the Smooth's "try anything" nature.

CHARACTERISTICS

Jack Marvin quotes Lord Byron's affection for dogs:
"The poor dog: in life the firmest friend,
The first to welcome, foremost to defend;
Whose honest heart is still his master's own;
Who labours, fights, lives, breathes for him alone."

If asked, and I frequently am, what is the ideal dog—my quick and easy response is—a Smooth Fox Terrier. They are ideal because of their sensitivity to humans, their easy maintenance, their basic good health, their indomitable spirit, and their wonderful temperaments. I do not think more could be said about this wonderful breed. Having a Smooth makes one's life and home complete.

Sometimes called the "ideal dog," Smooths are known for their sensitivity, even temperaments, and hardiness. Ch. Warfox Hilcrest Penny Prince, owned by Linda Nelson.

THE STANDARD FOR THE SMOOTH FOX TERRIER

In E. Lindley Wood's handbook, *Smooth Fox Terriers*, he recites the following poem as written by a former Secretary of the Kennel Club who sent it to the editor of the *Foxterrier Chronicle* in 1893.

Ch. Son of Tomahawk, owned by Donna Procyson-Hodgson.

"Head long and lean, with skull very flat;
Neck strong and clean set on shoulders, that
Are sloping with plenty of freedom;
Ears should be small, V-shaped as well,
Eyes small and keen, and clear as a bell,
And chiselled out neatly beneath 'em.
Although they should cover plenty of ground,
With well-sprung ribs and barrel round,
Their back should be but a short one;
Muscular quarters, hocks low and bent,

Tail thick, and carried as if they meant
business when they were called on.
Forelegs very straight, not bossy outside;
Chest giving heart room, but must not be wide:
With coat close and dense, and a hard one;
Then I think you will have one, to gallop and stay,
Through plough, cold and wet, to the end of the day,
And one you have cause to be proud on!"

The AKC first approved a written standard for the Smooth Fox Terrier in 1876. This is Ch. Talbach Tomahawk Medicine Man, owned by Donna Procyson-Hodgson.

The American Kennel Club approved a written standard for the Smooth Fox Terrier in 1876 that had been proposed by its breed-defending denizens from the American Fox Terrier Club. The language was taken exactly from the written standard of the English Kennel Club and adopted by the AFTC. In reading the standard one must appreciate the writing style of those authors so many years ago. Their ability to turn a phrase that aids in clarity of definition and allows a mental picture to develop is a changing art today.

In February 1967 Terence Bresnahan, noted terrier authority, judge and artist, judged the AFTC Specialty, that was at one time held in conjunction with the Westminster Kennel Club show, and, according to Eleanor Gilbert in the July 1967 issue of *Popular Dogs* magazine, he had this to say: "I had the greatest collection of Wires and Smooths in a ring at one time that I have ever seen in my life. It was a great thrill." He continues, "…type…is a compact body, properly stationed, not too high, not too low, in stance, the feet covering a lot of ground. The head is carried elegantly through the proper neck. For the future, new people coming into the game must get this picture of the proper Fox Terrier. They must learn to see the whole dog which should be in balance. They do not want to see this beautiful head and forget all about the rest of the dog. You can get the greatest expression in the world but yet the dog can be no good if it is not properly balanced.

"When you have a compact Fox Terrier, you have a great amount of energy in a small package, a square build, as the Standard says, height at the withers and length of body from shoulder-point to buttock - the ideal when the last two measurements are the same."

"So people coming into the game now have to develop a proper eye for Fox Terriers. Fox Terriers differ from all other terriers in the group. We must not

The breed standard defines what the "ideal" Smooth Fox Terrier should look like. Ch. Talbach Trusty Tomahawk, owned by Donna Procyson-Hodgson.

have a Lakeland. A Welsh can never be a Fox Terrier. All these square-built dogs must be distinguished one from the other, as each is different.

"Exaggeration is a great mistake. When any part is exaggerated, you are spoiling the dog. Exaggeration means that part is out of balance with the rest of the dog. Using the head for measurement, it should fit into every other part of the dog, such as from the occiput down to the withers; so much of the head-length from the withers to the base of the tail. Then, so much of the

head from the withers down to the depth of the ribs; from the elbow down to the feet, and on through the rest of body's various measurements.

"The dog must have a good, clean, refined head, and this head must not be on the shoulders. It must be well-separated by a good, strong, well-arched neck that goes into the shoulders properly.

"And we must say that a dog is well-coupled-up. We must distinguish between a dog and a bitch. We must have the depth of rib, and, one very important thing, we must have the forechest! There are many terriers today that are pigeon- or chicken-breasted. This depth of rib is very important, and it must come in

A promising Smooth Fox Terrier puppy can be anything you desire: a champion, companion dog, therapy dog, and more—but definitely a best friend!

front, too. This provides good lung and heart room, the well-developed forechest.

"The Fox Terrier should be well-rounded in flesh, not a bulbous thing, but distinctly not of a narrow, racy build.…If you get too long and lean a head, you are apt to get a racy dog which is a little bit leggy and with too much length of back. It should be well-rounded in flesh and have good substance. While we want no sign of raciness, we do not want a dog which is too coarse. There must be refinement there."

The following is the American Kennel Club standard for the Smooth Fox Terrier, with the author's clarification following in italics. Any deviation from these statements in the standard is not acceptable.

Smooth Fox Terriers can only become show dogs when they are good examples of the breed according to the standard.

General Appearance—The dog must present a generally gay, lively and active appearance: bone and strength in a small compass are essentials; but this must not be taken to mean that a Fox Terrier should be cloddy, or in any way coarse - speed and endurance must be looked to as well as power, and the symmetry of the Foxhound taken as a model. The Terrier, like the Hound, must on no account be leggy, nor must he be too short in the leg. He should stand like a cleverly made hunter, covering a lot of ground,

The standard clearly states that the Smooth Fox is "generally gay, lively, and active in appearance." Bowmanor's Johnson, owned by Richard and Linda Mote, is ready for a romp in the snow.

yet with a short back, as stated below. He will then attain the highest degree of propelling power, together with the greatest length of stride that is compatible with the length of his body. Weight is not a certain criterion of a Terrier's fitness for his work—general shape, size and contour are the main points; and if a dog can gallop and stay, and follow his fox up a drain, it matters little what his weight is to a pound or so.

N.B. Old scars or injuries, the result of work or accident, should not be allowed to prejudice a Terrier's chance in the show ring, unless they interfere with its movement or with its utility for work or stud.

Gay and lively—think of a dog bounding up and down in place with excitement, tail flailing back and forth, literally grinning from ear to ear, with ears flying up and back down with each leap—that is the joyous picture one must grasp of a Smooth Fox Terrier. This is a breed that is happy and totally guileless. There are no dark sides, no moody moments, no preconceived notions—they merely take it for what it appears to be without looking for the real reason. However, do not let this "Peter Pan" on four legs fool you into believing they are not intent, determined, cleverly wily and ready for the foray when necessary. Contrary to the Wire, they do not go looking for a fight, but will defend their ground with equal resilience.

Size, Proportion, Substance—According to present-day requirements, a full-sized, well balanced dog should not exceed 15 $\frac{1}{2}$ inches at the withers—the bitch being proportionately lower—nor should the length of back from withers to root of tail exceed 12 inches, while to maintain the relative proportions, the head should not exceed 7 $\frac{1}{4}$ inches or be less than 7 inches. A dog with these measurements should scale 18 pounds in show condition—a bitch weighing some two pounds less—with a margin of one pound either way.

Balance—This may be defined as the correct proportions of a certain point or points, when considered in relation to a certain other point or points. It is the keystone of the Terrier's anatomy. The chief points for consideration are the relative proportions of skull and foreface; head and back; height at withers; and length of body from shoulder-point to buttock—the ideal of proportion being reached when the last two measurements are the same. It should be added that, although the head measurement can be taken with absolute accuracy, the height at withers and length of back and coat are approximate, and are inserted for the information of breeders and exhibitors rather than as a hard-and-fast rule.

An important consideration when selecting a Smooth Fox is balance. Are all the parts of the dog in proportion to one another? Ch. Son of Tomahawk, owned by Donna Procyson-Hodges.

A Smooth Fox Terrier is a square dog. It is as simple as that. A somewhat longer back, a length usually found in the loin area, is more acceptable in a bitch.

However, there is no open-ended tolerance of length of body. The criteria is spelled out in the standard for correct size, with points ascertaining balance so clearly defined as to leave no question of expectation in the breeder's or judge's mind. As for the head, an overly long head usually goes with an unattractive long back, and therein loses the essence of the Smooth. In the Wire Standard it refers to a head that is exceptionally long with a short body, as something one might consider "a freak." With coat and beard not available for enhancements or hiding flaws, one must be even more watchful and demanding for the proper length of head in a Smooth.

Head—Eyes and **rims** should be dark in color, moderately small and rather deep set, full of fire, life and intelligence and as nearly possible circular in shape. Anything approaching a yellow eye is most objectionable. **Ears** should be V-shaped and small, of moderate thickness, and dropping forward close to the cheek, not hanging by the side of the head like a Foxhound. The topline of the folded ear should be well above the level of the skull.

The eyes of the Smooth Fox Terrier are deep set and should convey intelligence, life, and spirit. The hard, steely, cool look of a Smooth can't be avoided.

Disqualifications—Ears prick, tulip or rose.

The ***skull*** should be flat and moderately narrow, gradually decreasing in width to the eyes. Not much "stop" should be apparent, but there should be more dip in the profile between the forehead and the top jaw than is seen in the case of a Greyhound. It should be noticed that although the foreface should gradually taper from eye to muzzle and should tip slightly at its junction with the forehead, it should not "dish" or fall away quickly below the eyes, where it should be full and well made up, but relieved from "wedginess" by a little delicate chiseling. There should be apparent little difference in length between the skull and foreface of a well balanced head. *Cheeks* must not be full.

The head of the Smooth Fox Terrier must be well balanced and in proportion to the rest of the dog.

Jaws, upper and lower, should be strong and muscular and of fair punishing strength, but not so as to resemble the Greyhound or modern English Terrier. There should not be much falling away below the eyes. This part of the head should, however, be moderately chiseled out, so as not to go down in a straight slope like a wedge. The *nose*, towards which the muzzle must gradually taper, should be black.

Disqualifications—Nose white, cherry or spotted to a considerable extent with either of these colors. The *teeth* should be as nearly as possible together, i.e., the points of the upper (incisors) teeth on the

A dog's bite is very important to his health. The Smooth's teeth should be together as nearly as possible.

outside or slightly overlapping the lower teeth. *Disqualifications*—Much undershot, or much overshot.

The head and all its parts make up the Fox Terrier. Without the keen expression, the appropriate placement of eyes, the near equal length of skull and foreface, planes of the head, and strength of jaw, there is no Fox Terrier. The hard, steely, cool look of a Smooth can't be avoided. With a Smooth, one can be dismissed just as quickly as one can be overwhelmed with love. These emotions will be found in the "hard-bitten" look. It is of utmost importance that the eyes are placed correctly to prevent an Asian or "spacy" look. This is an animal that looks straight on at things. There is no dreamy "tomorrow" look or attitude about a Smooth. If the situation comes up, then now is the time to deal with it.

To frame the picture of the head of a Smooth correctly, one must look at the ears. They must fold and break above the skull, and hang forward, preferably not large. Anything else ruins the picture.

Neck, Topline, Body—*Neck* should be clean, muscular, without throatiness, of fair length, and gradually widening to the shoulders. ***Back*** should be short, straight, (i.e., level), and strong, with no appearance of slackness. *Chest* deep and not broad. *Brisket* should be deep, yet not exaggerated. The foreribs should be moderately arched, the back ribs deep and well sprung, and the dog should be well ribbed up. *Loin* should be very powerful, muscular and very slightly arched. ***Stern*** should be set on rather high, and carried gaily, but not over the back or curled. It should be of good strength, anything approaching a "Pipestopper" tail being especially objectionable.

In a Smooth, the arch and length of neck is vastly important. There should be no ugly hidden ghosts in the clean lines of a Smooth's neck and topline—what you see is what you get. Certainly, there are techniques for enhancement of a Smooth's coat, but not with the flexibility of a Wire. It is absolutely a demand for a Smooth to have a level topline. The slight rise

The proper tail or stern is of utmost importance, it actually predicts the true ability of this animal to function.

over the loin is basically one of musculature and adds strength and flexibility to the rear—the better to push in the hole after the critter, as well as being valuable for scampering back out!

The chest is deep, but certainly not wide—the use of the words "not exaggerated" are right on the money.

The proper tail or stern is the telltale, or tail, if you will, for the true ability of this animal to function. Where the tail comes out of the dog is vitally important.

Generally, a lower tail set establishes that the entire rear assembly is a bit more under the dog. The rear extension is not as dramatic as it could be, thus the forward movement is not as forceful. The thickness of the tail should balance the bone and body mass of the Smooth, it should be stiff, and with appropriate slight angle toward the head. The tail also is a forewarning of the current attitude of the dog.

The Fox Terrier tail is docked for a reason, and not merely to satisfy the aesthetics of early preponents of the breeds. When the terrier goes into the hole, he frequently gets his teeth on something equal to his own size, and it would become quite a feat of strength to get back out of the burrow dragging a fighting, kicking mad mass of vengeance without a little assistance from his master. Therefore, the thinnest, tender portion of the tail was snipped off to allow a man's hand to grab only the thick, sturdy part and thus, help pull the two opponents out.

It does not hurt the dog, and he actually expects it. In the show ring, many handlers will start a gait with a quick lift of the rear by the tail which seems to excite the Smooth into more eagerness. Merely a trick of the trade!

Forequarters—*Shoulders* should be long and sloping, well laid back, fine at the points, and clearly cut at the withers. The elbows should hang perpendicular to the body, working free of the sides. The forelegs viewed from any direction should be straight with bone strong right down to the feet, showing little or no appearance of ankle in front, and being short and straight in pastern. Both fore and hind legs should be carried straight forward in traveling.

John Marvin, lawyer, writer, judge, terrier breeder, a man with a keen sense of evaluating dogs, and fortunately for me, a friend, had this to say in **The Fox Terrier Scrapbook** about shoulder and front assembly on a good fox terrier.

"The shoulders are long and sloping and fine at the points. This desideratum not only permits a long easy stride to help the dog cover ground but it adds greatly to the beauty of the animal. A well-fitted and properly-laid-back shoulder contributes much to the shortness and beauty of outline. The chest must be deep to afford adequate heart room but should not be broad. This is a requirement since a wide-fronted dog, as occasioned by a broad chest, does not meet the specifications for either work or show and often "paddles when moving."

On the other hand two front legs "coming out of the same hole" is equally distressing and generally causes the dog to "weave" when moving.

Jake Terhune (a handler in the 30s & 40s) said so aptly of a dog too narrow in front, "when he comes to you he looks like he's knitting a sweater."

The forequarters of a Smooth Fox Terrier must allow the dog a long, easy stride, as well as adding greatly to the beauty of the animal.

At this time it may be well to mention that well-laid-back shoulders suggest shoulder blades with properly proportioned upper arms resulting in front legs being set in under the body and not stuck on at the front end. A Fox Terrier, as with any other dog, should have something in front of his legs. The exaggerated and deplored Fox Terrier "front" caused by poor angulation and compensated through the shortened upper arm is an abomination. In this connection, this so-called modified "Terrier front" is discussed in McDowell Lyons' book, Dogs in Motion, and is stated as being the rule rather than the exception in long-legged Terriers. If it is, it should not be because the entire premise for its existence is based upon a fallacy. Lyons suggests that this modified front was bred into dogs to enable them to dig. It is submitted that few dogs of today ever dig within a fox earth, on the other hand dogs of yesteryear were actually used for this purpose.

To this end, the photograph of the skeleton of the great Belgrave Joe...it will be noted that the upper arm is every bit as long, if not a bit longer, than the shoulder blade, small solace for those who promote the modified front. Actually no dog could even approach the desideratum of resembling "a cleverly made hunter" with this abortive front so prevalent today. Such a modification makes "reaching out" an impossibility and is the reason why so many have so little drive and such stilty movement."

Feet should be round compact, and not large; the soles hard and tough; the toes moderately arched, and turned neither in nor out.

Hindquarters—Should be strong and muscular, quite free from droop or crouch; the thighs long and powerful, the stifles well curved and turned neither in nor out; the hock well bent and near the ground should be perfectly upright and parallel each with the other when viewed from behind, the dog standing well up on them like a Foxhound, and not straight in the stifle. The worst possible form of hindquarters consists of a short second thigh and a straight stifle. Both fore and hind legs should be carried straight forward in traveling, the stifles not turning outward. Feet as in front.

Coat—Should be smooth, flat, but hard, dense and abundant. The belly and underside of the thighs should not be bare.

Color—White should predominate; brindle, red, or

liver markings are objectionable. Otherwise this point is of little or no importance.

White must predominate in this breed; however, where the color is placed on the dog is of little consequence. Except in the instance of an ill-placed marking that can cause an adverse look to a Smooth's construction, a situation more uncomely in a Smooth than Wire. For example, a spot of color undesirably located high on the withers will make a dog's neck look short, his back long, and will give the appearance of insufficient arch to the neck and an unsmooth gradual slope into the topline.

Gait—Movement, or action, is the crucial test of conformation. The terrier's legs should be carried straight forward while traveling, the forelegs handing perpendicular and swinging parallel to the sides, like the pendulum of a clock. The principal propulsive power is furnished by the hind legs, perfection of action being found in the terrier possessing long thighs and muscular second thighs well bent at the stifles, which admit of a strong forward thrust or "snatch" of the hocks. When approaching, the forelegs should form a continuation of the straight line of the front, the feet being the same distance apart as the elbows. When stationary it is often difficult to determine whether a dog is slightly out at shoulder, but, directly he moves, the defect—if it exists—becomes

Even as a puppy, "Derek" shows good conformation and the easy stride Smooth Fox Terriers are known for.

more apparent, the fore-feet having a tendency to cross, "weave" or "dish." When, on the contrary, the dog is tied at the shoulder, the tendency of the feet is to move wider apart, with a sort of paddling action. When the hocks are turned in - cow hocks - the stifles and feet are turned outwards, resulting in a serious loss of propulsive power. When the hocks are turned outwards the tendency of the hind feet is to cross, resulting in an ungainly waddle.

White should be the predominant color of the Smooth's coat. Markings are of little consequence except if they are ill placed and cause the dog to appear malformed.

When looking at a Smooth one must recognize that the length of the first and second thigh bones are

almost equal, the pelvic assembly is lifted very slightly, and there is moderate angulation—all of these things in place, you will then have that push of hock that ejects the dog forward. Further, the standard requires short hocks and long thighs. If one selects a dog with a very long thigh and very short hocks, the dog will not be a correct interpretation of the standard, and, fur-

ther, will be unable to function properly. The hocks must be straight up and down and not wing out, nor be at an angle so that the toes are under the body as opposed to being straight under the hock.

A word about "moderate" angulation is necessary. To some the word moderate means slight to less. To some it means usual or deliberate. You can quickly understand why there is a wide range of angulation seen in the ring today. One must compare breeds known for their extreme rear angles to put in perspective the functioning meaning of "moderate" for a Smooth Fox Terrier. On a scale from one to ten, we can get a better feel for "moderate." A Chinese Shar Pei is a guard dog and must be able to stand his ground very solidly. His rear is not designed for briskly running through the hunting fields. Therefore, his rear angulation does not have the same requirements of a Smooth—he is more straight, with very little angulation and could be labeled a "2," "3," or as much as a "4" on our scale of angulation. However, guess what the Chinese Shar Pei's standard states its requirements are in regard to the rear: "moderately angulated.' In my opinion, a Smooth must have an adequate amount of angulation for both digging, returning from the hole, running with the hounds and stamina. Ergo, a Fox Terrier would be classified as a "5," "6," or even a "7," but no more. In other words, as a Fox Terrier judge and breeder, I appreciate "more" than "less."

The overall appearance of a Smooth Fox Terrier when stacked should illustrate all of the breed standard as a whole.

Bounding through the fields, this Smooth Fox puppy takes the standard illustration for temperament to heart!

Temperament—The dog must present a generally gay, lively and active appearance.

Disqualifications—Ears prick, tulip or rose. Nose white, cherry or spotted to a considerable extent with either of these colors. Mouth much undershot, or much overshot.

The standard has been clearly stated in a booklet produced by The American Fox Terrier Club, which definitively states what is expected in a Smooth.

You should contact the American Kennel Club, 51 Madison Avenue, New York, NY 10010 for the address of the current club secretary to obtain this inexpensive booklet.

HISTORY OF THE SMOOTH FOX TERRIER

Since before time there has been a straight-legged, clean-lined, rectangle-headed, wolf-like cur. With a little imagination, it is not difficult to perform a mental exercise that would take one's mind from that early creature to the dogs of today.

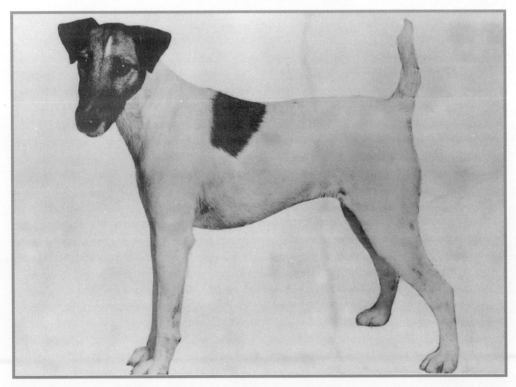

The Smooth Fox Terrier is a multi-faceted breed, able to be all things to all people, an all-around excellent animal.

The end result could be a Smooth Fox Terrier—an easy progression. This is a breed that is all things—a dog's dog, a man's dog, a family choice, a working dog, and, in fact, a general, all-round excellent animal. Irving C. Ackerman's book, *The Complete Fox Terrier*, sums up the Fox Terrier as follows:

"So fascinating is the Fox Terrier breed, so responsive is the dog, so ready for fight or frolic, so classical in his outline, that it is seldom indeed that anybody ever deserts the breed for another.

"Often enough I have been asked to state my reasons for my preference for Fox Terriers over other dogs.

I like all kinds of dogs, but the Fox Terrier appeals to me especially because: He possesses such perfect symmetry in so small a compass - a veritable *multum in parvo*.

"He is, indoors or out, a bright trappy, and merry companion, keen for a romp, a hike or a motor ride.

"He is a great little workman, a destroyer *par excellence* of vermin - fox, badger, stoat, weasel, rabbit, mole and rat.

"He is level-headed, loyal, intelligent and dead game; yet withal kind, gentle and tractable.

Smooth Fox Terriers are so responsive that they inspire an almost feverish loyalty in their owners.

"He is easy to teach anything any dog can learn, and can do not only his own particular work but also the work of spaniel, retriever, or other hunting dog, on land or in water.

"He is easily reared, and has the stamina to "fight through" illnesses and injuries.

"The cost of feeding and housing him is small.

"There is a steady market for surplus puppies of well-bred stock.

"He breeds dead-true to type, enabling the breeder to reap the fruits of his knowledge and to observe the results of his errors of judgment in the arrangement of matings.

"He is a grand little showman; and when he goes into the ring with his head erect and his flag flying he is as proud of you at one end of the lead as you are of him at the other.

"And, lastly, the cult of the Fox Terrier has attracted to it fine sportsmen and sportswomen, hospitable, generous, loyal to their breed, and good fellows, win, lose or draw."

However, John T. Marvin puts it in a more succinct manner in *The Fox Terrier Scrapbook* as adapted

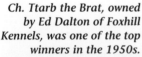

Ch. Ttarb the Brat, owned by Ed Dalton of Foxhill Kennels, was one of the top winners in the 1950s.

Fox Terriers are known throughout history as hunting dogs that "go to ground" after vermin. Today there are trials for dogs trained in this sport.

from a poem found in Reverend Skinner's book:

"Full of fire and Strong of bone
With background old and fathers known
Fine his nose, with nostrils thin,
But blown abroad by pride within.
His neck is like a river flowing,
Eyes deepset like embers glowing,
Fearless, seeing day or night,
And paced by movement swift as light."

The Smooth and Wire Fox Terriers were liberally interbred until recently. Having established the desired type, purists of the two sister breeds felt the intercrossing of both gene pools weakened the credibility of each distinct variety. It is the American way to recognize the specialist in any field—why not dogs?

Artwork of the Roman times shows Caesar, after conquering Britain, with small dogs that go to ground. This indicates the antiquity of Fox Terriers. Dr. John Caius, a physician, presented a book, in 1557 in Latin, *English Dogges*, that mentions a hunting dog that "hunteth the Foxe and the Badger or Greye onely, whom we call Terrars, because they (after the manner and customs of ferrets in searching for Connyes (rabbits), creepe into the grounde and by that means make afrayde, nyppe and byte the Foxe and the Badger in such sort, that eyther they teare them in pieces with theyr teeth beying in the bosome of the earth or else hayle and pull them perforce out of their lurking angles, darke dongeons and close cayes, or at the least through conceived feare drive them out of their hollow harbours, in so much that they are com-

It is believed that the Smooth is the product of crossing the smooth coated terrier of Wales, Derbyshire, and Durham, the Bullterrier, the Greyhound, and the Beagle.

pelled to prepare speedie flyte, and being desirous of the next (albeit not the safest) refuse, are otherwise taken and intrapped with snares and nettes layde over holes to the same purpose."

In today's world, these are harsh words indeed, but one must understand that in those days, survival depended not on a nine-to-five job, but in the sole responsibility of providing a livelihood for one's family from the land, and the hunting grounds at one's disposal. Life itself was not easy—there was certainly no two weeks vacation with pay!

The Latin word terra means earth, and thus this dog, who feared nothing, would go into the holes in the dark ground to aid the farmer or landsmen in getting rid of pests that would destroy his crop. Or perhaps he gave chase to help catch the natural food that fed his family. And so he was given the name that most aptly applied to his work—Terrier.

There are those who believe the Smooth Fox Terrier was developed prior to its sister breed, the Wire, by a decade or more. One's common sense would tell us that it stands to reason the smooth coat would more likely be the default in animals, rather than a wire coat. However, one must understand that the Wire Fox Terrier came from a "rough-haired" colored dog and was not the beautifully, albeit contrived, groomed jacket we know today. Beauty in this little working fellow was secondary to his ability to hunt.

It is believed that the Smooth is the development of crossings between the old black and tan, smooth-coated terrier of Wales, Derbyshire and Durham, the Bullterrier, the Greyhound and the Beagle. Considering the temperament, abilities and appearance of the Smooth, it is readily apparent that all the characteristics of these breeds compiled favorably into one dog—the Smooth Fox Terrier.

With the Smooth's keen nose, ability to give voice as to where his prey is hiding, his running stamina, and his capacity for warm bonding as a family pet, the Smooth has made good use of the collective gene pool. In Mr. Ackerman's book he states, "The wire-haired terrier was larger, more powerful and harden bitten; the smooth haired, more stylish and considerably smaller, nevertheless larger than the standard calls for today."

The Smooth, with his white coat, was more appealing to the hunter, as a dog of red or black-and-brown coat could easily be mistaken for the very thing they hunted—the fox.

Not until 1876 was a standard for the Fox Terrier drawn up, and until that time dogs were bred by using a flight of fancy method. Some of the pre-standard terriers who helped create the specific Fox Terrier line were Old Jock, Old Trap and Old Tarter all born around 1860. It is from this trio the make and shape of Smooth Fox Terriers originated. Old Jock was more like the modern Smooth, and was nearly 18 pounds, but with a shorter head, and was a handy winner at the competitions. At ten years of age he was defeated by Old Tarter, who was more of the Bullterrier type, and quite game. Old Trap was 27 pounds, had tremendous substance and a long head. According to Ackerman, Old Trap was well liked by the terrier clan of the day who called him "the vest-pocket Hercules." Later, Belvoir Joe produced Belgrave Joe in 1868, who lived nearly 20 years, and is considered one of the most influential Smooths in early history. Descending from these roots are Rattler (1871) or "the dreaded Rattler" as he was called, and Old Foiler, who attracted the eye of Frances Redmond, a name that was to figure heavily in the future of the Smooth.

The Smooth possesses a keen nose, the ability to give voice as to where his prey is hiding, running stamina, and the capacity to bond with his family.

According to some students of the breed, Foiler is the result of a very tight pedigree of Grove Tartar to Grove Nettle, that produced Grove Willie and Grove Vixen. Breeding this brother and sister together produced Grip and Juddy (Judy) who produced Foiler. One would be very hesitant to make public an attempt at that type of inbreeding today.

One of the early breeders of Fox Terriers was The Rev. John Russell (1795-1883) who founded the Jack Russell Terrier, a breed still available today. Foiler's dam was of Jack Russell descent, and from that came Dickon who was the roots of Vicary's Vesuvian and New Forest, the foundation stock for Sir Frances Redmond. Mr. Redmond is credited with taking a "throw-away" puppy from a siring of Tartar and creating the beautiful type of Smooth known today. Mr. Redmond, who was quite a young man when he became interested in the Fox Terrier, had been bitten by the dog show bug. In 1872 he entered his first show with his new strain of Smooth Fox Terriers. His goal was to breed true a Smooth with sound, straight legs and good, proper feet. Some years later, after a rather slow start, he produced nine champions in only one year, an unheard of precedent, thus proving it could and should be done. Mr. Redmond built his kennel on three extremely sound bitches: Dame Fortune, Duchess of Durham and Donna Fortuna—all champions.

Another famous breeder of those early years was Robert Vicary. Combining the Redmond-Vicary bloodlines, breeders and followers who came later recognized the value being produced by these two antago-

The Smooth Fox Terrier gained popularity as a hunting dog, in part, because of his white coat which makes him easily distinguishable from prey.

nists and made great use of the bloodlines, which proved very fruitful. One such joining was the bitch from Mr. Redmond's line, Ch. Donna Fortuna, who was never defeated at a show. According to Sidney Castle in the sixth edition of *Our Dogs*, she was a masculine, fairly large bitch, and was hailed as near perfection. When she was bred to Mr. Vicary's Dreadnought, that mating produced one of the best

The 1950s produced a kennel that was to become one of the greatest in America—Foxden, owned by Mr. and Mrs. James Farrell. Pictured here is Foxden Nightshade Lady.

known Smooths—a bitch named Ch. The Sylph - a glorious example of the Smooth Fox Terrier.

From those early efforts come the three outstanding lines that contribute to today's version of a Smooth Fox Terrier, that eventually brings us to the dog all Americans hold as the greatest Smooth of all time. This one Smooth is the mold that breeders, still today, set as their ultimate breeding goal—Ch. Nornay Saddler.

There are three Smooths that history believes began the Nornay ultimate success story. They were Orluke, Southboro Sandman and Cromwell Ocre. All three were sons of Orkadian. When bred, these three sires produced progeny that was so outstanding, the study of their line will prove most educational. A mere five or six generations forward will bring one to an interesting pedigree—not necessarily tightly bred, but none the less, one of such a dominate gene pool as to be the entire basis for the American Smooth Fox Terrier. Eng. Ch. Selecta Ideal when bred to Eng. Ch. Viva produced Eng.Ch.Verily, and when Eng. Ch. Selecta Ideal was bred to Eng. Avon Snowflake, Eng. Ch. Avon Starling was produced - all of English bloodlines.

Not until 1876 was a standard written for the Smooth Fox Terrier. Before this time dogs were bred by a "flight of fancy" method—different litters resembled different contributing ancestors.

Combining those with Eng. Ch. Avon Peddlar, Yours Truly, Bowden Constable and Eng. Ch. Bowden Rakishly, they produced Eng. Ch. Travelling Fox and Wyrksop Surprise, and it is from that glorious mating that we get Eng/Am. Ch. Nornay Saddler. He was not only a dog of near perfect proportions and wonderful attitude, but a preponent sire that started Americans on a love affair with the Smooth Fox Terrier. If, as a novice, you would rather not reveal your newcomer status, merely mention *the Saddler* in reverenced tones, and you will be immediately accepted into the encircling arms of the Fox Terrier fancy. There is a magnificent replica of Saddler in oil by Edwin Megargee, an American artist (1883-1958). If you would like to see this picture of *Saddler*, you may do so on the electronic network. The address is http://www.akc.org/akcart1.htm. Visiting the AKC on the web is a very interesting trip for additional artwork, current news, forms, questions and answers.

Joyfield's Marco and the Khan and Balboa on the Beach owned by Linda Sallee-Hill.

There also are many kennels, breeders, and dogs that should be recognized for their contribution to the development of the Smooth. Her Grace, Kathleen Duchess of Newcastle (Of Notts - both Wires and Smooths), Mrs. T. Losco Bradley (Cromwell), Mr. Calvert Butler (Watteau, both Wires and Smooths), and his daughter, Mrs. Mary Blake, who has continued the Watteau Smooth bloodlines, Sir Frances Redmond (Totteridge and Dusky), Mrs. Bennett Edwards (owned Doncaster Dominie), Mr. Reeks (owned Avon Oxendale), and Mr. Bradley (owned Cromwell Ochre). Without these breeders who were willing to share their established bloodlines with the "Yanks," the quality of Smooth Fox Terriers would not be as advanced and stable as it is today.

THE SMOOTH IN AMERICA

The American Fox Terrier Club was established in 1886 with the English Kennel Club's standard for the Fox Terrier set in place. Only the weight changed from those early days of a larger, leggier dog, down to 18 pounds, which is the current requirement.

After *Saddler*, the American Smooth took off with enthusiasm and joy. Those early American breeders who did well for and with the breed include Mrs. Barbara Lowe Fallas (Andely Kennels), who in 1939, based her successful kennel on Buckland and Avon Bondette. Mrs. Fallas finished 39 champions, 31 of which she bred. It is through Mrs. Fallas that the Georgia kennel of Norman, Mary and Chris Bowker (Bowmanor) got their start with a bitch who still holds the record of being one of the all-time top producers - Bowmanor's Dolly of Beafox. It is said this bitch could be bred to a rabbit and produce champion Smooths!

In the 1910 decade Mr. F. H. Farwell of Texas (Sabine Kennels) produced Ch. Sabine Rarebit, Ch. Sabine Rifle, and Ch. Sabine Forever. It was Ch. Sabine Forever who was the first American bred dog to become an English champion. It seems the tables were turning!

Mr. Farwell wanted only black and white Smooths, as he believed the browns muddied the gene pool. He started with Eng. Ch. Ridgewood Result and, as was acceptable in those early days, changed his name to Sabine Result. Result dominated the show ring for many years. Mr. Farwell finished some 40 champions and his Sabine name can still be seen in the back generations of current pedigrees. He sold Ch. Sabine

Fernlike to Thomas Varick, who put a respectable winning record on the dog.

Other producers during the 1930s were Ch. Brass Tacks, owned by Jere Collins, Ch. Nornay Saddler, owned by James Austin, Ch. Fancy That, owned by H. Cota, Farleton Foxearth, imported by the Wissaboo Kennel, and Buckland of Andely bred and owned by Barbara Lowe Fallas. In the 1940s, Mrs. Fallas was at her peak with Ch. She's Bonny of Andely, and Mr. Austin presented Ch. Full Measure of Wissaboo. William Brainard, who became an AKC judge in later years, won handily with Ch. Downsbragh Speak Easy. Additional breeders turned judges were Mr. and Mrs. Potter Wear of Stoney Meadows Kennels in Maryland.

The 1950s produced a kennel that was to become one of the greatest kennels on the American shore—Foxden, owned by Mr. and Mrs. James Farrell of the Farrell steamship lines. The Farrell's got their start when they imported Ch. Flornell Prestonian Jewel and have stated that Jewel was the greatest Smooth they ever had. This is quite a compliment, as over

The American Fox Terrier Club was established in 1886, using the English Kennel Club's standard.

To have bred the quality of dogs that Foxden is known for is truly outstanding, however, they also readily shared their dogs with other breeders to help them get started. Ch. Foxden Nighthawk at Missions owned by Linda Sallee-Hill.

some 40 years of involvement the Foxden Kennels produced many top-winning dogs as a result of that smart purchase. Some of their top winners include Foremark Ebony Box of Foxden, Foxden Fairy Godmother, Ellastone Fireflash, Karnilo Chieftain of Foxden, Foxden Warpaint and Foxden Warspite. To have bred the quality of dogs known at Foxden is a worthy statement, however, more recognizable was their willingness to share their good dogs with other breeders, thus helping them get started.

Other top winners of the time were Ch. Woodcliffe Hiya Boy (owner, Albert Welty), Ch. Mullantean Miss Florence (owner, Pat and Henry Speight, Jr.), Ch. Watteau Snufsed of Crag Crest (owner, Mr. and Mrs. Fred Kuska), Ch. Boreham Baranova (owner, Elsie Simmons), Ch. Boreham Bonanza (owner, Carlotta

Ch. Legacy Rex Morgansonne C.D., owned by Jack and Ruth Edwards.

Howard), Ch. Toofox the Caribe Chief Spy (owner, Joe and Murrel Purkhiser of Texas), Ch. Foxmoor Macho Macho Man (owner, Harold Nedell), and the indomitable Australian import, Ch. Ttarb the Brat owned by Ed Dalton of Foxhill Kennels.

There are many breeders who must be acknowledged for their dedication to showing quality dogs weekend after weekend, improving the breed, creating the dream and justifing their creativity in the whelping box. Some of these include: Madison Weeks, now an AKC judge, Hugh Thomas, Waybroke Kennels of Florida, Winifred H. Stout (Quissex Kennels in Rhode Island), Mr. and Mrs. William E. Dossett, whose most noteworthy Smooths are Ch. Toofox White Hunter and Ch. Toofox Chief Spy of the Toofox Kennels of Arizona, Richard and Virginia Ashlock, owners of Ch. Laurelton Now or Never (Laurelton Kennels of California), Jane Swanson (Foxtrot Kennels of Illinois), and Nance and Michael Buckley (Buckleigh Kennel of New Hampshire). Mr. and Mrs. Buckley have bred several top winning dogs including: Ch. Buckleigh New Kid on the Block, Ch. Buckleigh Anticipation, and Ch. Buckleigh Captain Fantastic.

Much thanks is owed to breed enthusiasts like these, who are dedicated to the breed as well as show them weekend after weekend.

THE WESTMINSTER KENNEL CLUB

In an effort to explain the purpose and thus the importance of purebred dog shows, George Frank Skelly in his book, *All About Fox Terriers*, states in cryptic and clear language the heart of a dog show.

"Dog shows, as most breeders recognize, are designed primarily for the purpose of selecting the better breeding specimens and only secondarily as sporting contest."

While his reference is to the Wire, his phraseology are words to live by for a breeder of any breed.

Since its inception in 1907, the Westminster Kennel Club has been and continues to be the culmination of one's ultimate creative breeding and exhibiting skills.

This elegant two-day show held in New York in February at the Madison Square Garden, is the place a student of any breed must attend. Dog aficionados

The Smooth Fox Terrier enjoys a high place of honor among Westminster Kennel Club alumni, as being the first winner of Best-in-Show in 1907.

from all over the world attend this nationally televised show, and even if there is a language barrier, the appreciation of the premier quality of dogs exhibited breaks through for clear mutual understanding. This show, due to space limitations, is for champions only. The judges are dressed in their best in long gowns and tuxedos, and recognition of the previous year's top winners are enjoyed at several exquisite parties. It is truly a high honor to be invited to judge at this prestigious show.

Many breed specialties are held prior to the kennel club's show, and the American Kennel Club, at 51 Madison Avenue, opens its doors to visitors who would like to enjoy the library and magnificent artwork, not to mention a chance to hob-knob with the powers-that-be at the kennel club.

The Smooth enjoys a high place of honor in Westminster history, for it was a Smooth Fox Terrier that won the first Westminster show in 1907. Winthrop Rutherford (Warren Kennels), a gentleman who held the breed close to his heart and proudly exhibited what he bred, won with Ch. Warren Remedy. If that wasn't enough for a show entered largely by sporting dogs, Remedy won again in 1908 and 1909. In 1910, the Kennels of Sabine owned by Mr. F. H. Farwell of Texas won with Ch. Sabine Rarebit.

However, it appears from this time on, the *Wire* Fox Terrier stole the scene at Westminster by winning Best in Show 13 times. While the Smooth may not be

The Smooth is one of the most popular breeds in the country with an appreciative audience worldwide.

The Montgomery County Kennel Club show began in 1929 as a specialty for terriers only. It is an annual celebration that attracts terrier students from all over the world. Maybe this dam's pup will appear there someday.

dressed in the fancy garb of his sister breed, he is still one of the most popular breeds in the country with an appreciative audience worldwide.

MONTGOMERY COUNTY KENNEL CLUB

George Frank Skelly, in his book *All About Fox Terriers*, recognized the true meaning of the sport of showing dogs, and stated: "Dog shows, as most breeders recognize, are designed primarily for the purpose of selecting the better breeding specimens and only secondarily as sporting contest.

Hence, in both theory and practice, a Wire fancier's success is best measured by ability to breed Wires of championship caliber."

And so it was that in 1915 a group of terrier people from an AKC member club in Pennsylvania named Gwynedd Valley Kennel Club met to formulate an all-terrier club and event. The Wissahickon Kennel Club, also in Pennsylvania, was a part of this development, as they too provided shows for terriers only. Through the cooperative efforts of these individuals involved in all three organizations, a tradition began they could not know would become the culmination of all terrier stardom in the US.

A happy, spirited companion, the Smooth Fox Terrier is truly a joy to own.

The terrier world, a close-knit, family-minded group of people, held its first Montgomery County Kennel Club show in 1929 for terrier breeds only. The annual celebration of this event has attracted terrier students from Japan, Australia, Russia, Sweden and all parts of the world to attend its show, now held in Ambler, Pennsylvania. Most terrier breed clubs consider this show a Specialty, and provide a Sweepstakes competition for young dogs. The show culminates with a Best Brace in Show, and finally with the ultimate Best in Show—a top specimen chosen from the various breed winners. To have one's entry acknowledged with even a placement at this show is memorable. To be invited to judge this event is the highest of honors.

There have been four Smooths to go Best In Show at Montgomery County: 1938s Ch. Nornay Saddler, 1941s Ch. Desert Deputy, 1951s Ch. Downsbragh Two O'Clock Fox, and in 1966, Ch. Foremark Ebony Box of Foxden. I have attended Montgomery County shows for many years, and was fortunate to be at ringside again in October 1994, and watched the thrill of a tantalizing win for our Smooths.

This particular year a brace of identical Smooths won. They were so enticing with their matching solid black faces and white bodies, and tails that continuously wagged in sync, they were easily the audience's and judge's favorite. It is easy to see why this happy breed is such a part of the American way.

Smooth Fox Terriers enjoy the companionship of their own breed—perhaps you'll decide to own a pair— double the fun!

In 1990, The Smooth Fox Terrier Association of America was formed. Their purpose is to provide an opportunity for breeders and exhibitors to gather and discuss Smooth Fox Terrier development.

SMOOTH FOX TERRIER ASSOCIATION OF AMERICA

Although not fully established, a devoted gathering of Smooth breeders met in June 1990 at the St. Louis Fox Terrier Specialty and officially formed a society for Smooths. Prior to 1990 they held matches to foster interest, and continue to do so to maintain enthusiasm. Future meetings will be held in conjunction with the Fox Terrier specialties at Montgomery County Kennel Club show. Their intent is to provide an opportunity for breeders and exhibitors to get together and focus on conversation and development of the Smooth Fox Terrier.

SELECTING A SMOOTH FOX TERRIER

Life has its special moments—marriage proposals, the birth of a child or grandchild, and the selection of a new puppy. The heady responsibility of this decision cannot be made on a whim. This is a decision that must be made by the entire family. Some considerations should be: Is the yard fenced in or will someone

If you should decide to bring a puppy into your life, it is not a decision that should be taken lightly. Owning a puppy is a lot of hard work, there are definite considerations that will have to be discussed.

be required to take the puppy (who strangely enough will grow into an adult!) outdoors for exercise and "potty" breaks. Who will take on this task even in the rain, cold or snow? No Smooth should be left outside eternally—they enjoy the company of their family too much to deprive them of that and, with little training, they are excellent house guests. How do you feel about dog hair on the furniture and carpet? If you've just decorated your home in all white—please, rethink this purchase. A dog is supposed to bring joy - not misery. Who will be the primary caregiver?

Is your lifestyle or that of your family ready for a new addition? Will someone have the time and patience it takes to make your puppy into a fulfilled, happy, and well-trained member of your household?

Usually it's the mom. If so, is she eager for the puppy, or is she being led reluctantly by her family? She is the key to the success of this relationship. Have you chosen a veterinarian? What do you know about him/her—or is the clinic just close by? Where will the puppy sleep, and where will he sleep when he becomes an adult? While these questions are not intended as stumbling blocks, they must be addressed. A Smooth is a wonderful pet and deserves a home that welcomes him. He is smart, clean, loving to his family and friends, as well as a protective watch dog and ratter.

After you have found the breeder you would like to do business with, the opportunity should be made available to you to come and watch the puppies as they play together.

A Smooth Fox Terrier's breeding is of great importance. Do your homework. Research breeders in your area until you find one that you are comfortable doing business with. A Smooth purchased from a reputable breeder will be a wonderful pet— he is smart, clean, loving, and protective. Bowmanor's One and Only owned by Chris Bowker.

After choosing a breeder, an opportunity to visit the kennel and view a litter should be made available to you. Take careful notice of the things you see there. Are the puppies clean and healthy looking? Do they seem happy and well fed? Are there any sires or dams on the premises?

This will be a key to deciding the temperament, quality, and personality of the puppy that fits your needs. If you have a young child or children, you certainly don't want the most aggressive puppy in the litter. However, you don't want a puppy that is a shrinking violet and won't defend himself against a baby's innocent but hurtful hands. It is up to you to teach the puppy manners regarding how he lets it be known that he's being hurt.

Watch the puppies—which one plays independently without his littermates? Which one comes right up to you immediately? Is there one that is more willing to stay in your lap, or would he rather be down on the floor playing? After you are satisfied with the temperament of the pups, then look at the structure of the dog. Ask to see the dam and sire, if available. Look at the pedigree and see if there are many AKC champions, also look for line-breedings in the first three generations. There are three kinds of matings that can be done. Linebreeding is building on one ancestor, but the parents are little, if at all, related to each other through any other ancestors and may involve distant generations. Inbreeding generally means mating son to mother, father to daughter, brother to sister, or half-brother to half-sister. Family breeding, a term coined by Mr. Lloyd C. Brackett, author of many articles for *Dog World*, and breeder at Long-Worth German Shepherd Kennels, explains the term as the breeding of interrelated animals that does not entirely come under the full auspices of inbreeding or linebreeding. The advantage of linebreeding, a choice made by most conscientious breeders, is predictability in the get. One literally doubles up on the like genes from the parents—- whether they are good or bad.

Now you have selected the square puppy with the long head, short back, upright tail - only to be told that is pick of the litter and must be placed in a show home. First, pat yourself on the back for picking a "good un", as they say in England, then re-evaluate your willingness to become involved in the sport of exhibiting purebred dogs. Most breeders will not part with their pick bitch for any amount of money. However, you may be able to negotiate an agreement that will allow the breeder to have her cake and eat it too! Be willing to sign a statement agreeing to have the dog shown on a shared expense basis, which may include grooming costs, if you are unwilling to do it yourself, and a puppy or puppies back from the first litter. Encourage the breeder to select the stud, as she knows more of the history of her dogs, as well as which stud dogs are available that complement her bloodline and your puppy. Remember, there is a fee for using a stud dog,

Opposite: Once you find a puppy with a temperament that suits you, look at his conformation. Does it meet with the standard—square with a long head, short back, upright tail? Ask to see his pedigree.

As you watch the puppies play together notice several things—which puppies play independently, come right up to you, or run the other way? This will be key to deciding the temperament of each pup—then you can decide which is right for you.

Another consideration when choosing a puppy—companion or show dog? Are you willing to spend the time and money a show dog will require? Oftentimes the benefits will far out weigh the effort.

plus there are costs involved with raising a litter of puppies. But the delight, education, and experience your family will share with a litter of puppies is worth all costs.

Should you feel that a show puppy is out of the question for you, then re-evaluate the litter with less perfection in mind. If you have selected a reputable breeder, they will not try to sell you a sickly or unhealthy puppy without your full knowledge.

Contact the American Kennel Club for the name and address of the secretary of the American Fox Terrier Club of America, who will supply you with a list of breeders in your area. Better yet—find out when there is a dog show nearby, and what time Fox Terriers are to be shown. Go to several shows to learn as much as you can. Buying a puppy is not like buying a new computer; it is more like adopting a child, and the responsibility of caring for your new addition is strictly up to you.

YOUR PUPPY'S NEW HOME

Before making the trip to pick up your puppy, be sure to purchase the items you will need for his basic care. If you wait until his arrival at home, important things will be forgotten in all the excitement.

Before actually collecting your puppy, it is better that you purchase the basic items you will need in advance of the pup's arrival date. This allows you more opportunity to shop around and ensure you have exactly what you want rather than having to buy lesser quality in a hurry.

It is always better to collect the puppy as early in the day as possible. In most instances this will mean that the puppy has a few hours with your family before it is time to retire for his first night's sleep away from his former home.

If the breeder is local, then you may not need any form of box to place the puppy in when you bring him home. A member of the family can hold the pup in his lap—duly protected by some towels just in case the puppy becomes car sick! Be sure to advise the breeder at what time you hope to arrive for the puppy, as this will obviously influence the feeding of the pup that morning or afternoon. If you arrive early in the

If the trip home is a long one, be sure to give your puppy ample opportunity to stretch his legs as well as relieve himself.

day, then they will likely only give the pup a light breakfast so as to reduce the risk of travel sickness.

If the trip will be of a few hours duration, you should take a travel crate with you. The crate will provide your pup with a safe place to lie down and rest during the trip. During the trip, the puppy will no doubt wish to relieve his bowels, so you will have to make a few stops. On a long journey you may need a rest yourself, and can take the opportunity to let the puppy get some fresh air. However, do not let the puppy walk where there may have been a lot of other dogs because he might pick up an infection. Also, if he relieves his bowels at such a time, do not just leave the feces where they were dropped. This is the height of irresponsibility. It has resulted in many public parks and other places actually banning dogs. You can purchase poop-scoops from your pet shop and should have them with you whenever you are taking the dog out where he might foul a public place.

Your journey home should be made as quickly as possible. If it is a hot day, be sure the car interior is amply supplied with fresh air. It should never be too hot or too cold for the puppy. The pup must never be placed where he might be subject to a draft. If the journey requires an overnight stop at a motel, be aware that other guests will not appreciate a puppy crying half the night. You must regard the puppy as a baby and comfort him so he does not cry for long periods. The worst thing you can do is to shout at or smack him. This will mean your relationship is off to a really bad start. You wouldn't smack a baby, and your puppy is still very much just this.

ON ARRIVING HOME

By the time you arrive home the puppy may be very tired, in which case he should be taken to his sleeping area and allowed to rest. Children should not be allowed to interfere with the pup when he is sleeping. If the pup is not tired, he can be allowed to investigate his new home—but always under your close supervision. After a short look around, the puppy will no doubt appreciate a light meal and a drink of water. Do not overfeed him at his first meal because he will be in an excited state and more likely to be sick.

Although it is an obvious temptation, you should not invite friends and neighbors around to see the new arrival until he has had at least 48 hours in which to settle down. Indeed, if you can delay this longer then do so, especially if the puppy is not fully vaccinated. At the very least, the visitors might introduce some local bacteria on their clothing that the puppy is not immune to. This aspect is always a risk when a pup has been moved some distance, so the fewer people the pup meets in the first week or so the better.

By the time you arrive home your puppy will probably be tired and a little confused. Try not to overwhelm him—let him inspect his surroundings without the interference of too many people. Offer him a cool drink and a light meal and your puppy will probably settle in for a much needed nap.

DANGERS IN THE HOME

Your home holds many potential dangers for a little mischievous puppy, so you must think about these in advance and be sure he is protected from them. The more obvious are as follows:

Open Fires. All open fires should be protected by a mesh screen guard so there is no danger of the pup being burned by spitting pieces of coal or wood.

Electrical Wires. Puppies just love chewing on things, so be sure that all electrical appliances are neatly hidden from view and are not left plugged in when not in use. It is not sufficient simply to turn the plug switch to the off position—pull the plug from the socket.

Open Doors. A door would seem a pretty innocuous object, yet with a strong draft it could kill or injure a puppy easily if it is slammed shut. Always ensure there is no risk of this happening. It is most likely during warm weather when you have windows or outside doors open and a sudden gust of wind blows through.

Balconies. If you live in a high-rise building, obviously the pup must be protected from falling. Be sure

Believe it or not your home holds many dangers for a mischievous little puppy. It is often a good idea to "puppy-proof" your home before his arrival. Be aware, many situations can be dangerous to a puppy. "Emma Lee," owned by Marita McGrath.

Small children should be closely supervised when interacting with puppies. Both parties need to be taught the appropriate way to interact with one another.

he cannot get through any railings on your patio, balcony, or deck.

Ponds and Pools. A garden pond or a swimming pool is a very dangerous place for a little puppy to be near. Be sure it is well screened so there is no risk of the pup falling in. It takes barely a minute for a pup—or a child—to drown.

The Kitchen. While many puppies will be kept in the kitchen, at least while they are toddlers and not able to control their bowel movements, this is a room full of danger—especially while you are cooking. When cooking, keep the puppy in a play pen or in another room where he is safely out of harm's way. Alternatively, if you have a carry box or crate, put him in this so he can still see you but is well protected.

Be aware, when using washing machines, that more than one puppy has clambered in and decided to have a nap and received a wash instead! If you leave the washing machine door open and leave the room for any reason, then be sure to check inside the machine before you close the door and switch on.

Something as seemingly innocuous as common houseplants can hold grave danger for your new puppy. Many plants are poisonous to dogs if ingested.

Small Children. Toddlers and small children should never be left unsupervised with puppies. In spite of such advice it is amazing just how many people not only do this but also allow children to pull and maul pups. They should be taught from the outset that a puppy is not a plaything to be dragged about the home—and they should be promptly scolded if they disobey.

Children must be shown how to lift a puppy so it is safe. Failure by you to correctly educate your children about dogs could one day result in their getting a very nasty bite or scratch. When a puppy is lifted, his weight must always be supported. To lift the pup, first place your right hand under his chest. Next, secure the pup by using your left hand to hold his neck. Now you can lift him and bring him close to your chest. Never lift a pup by his ears and, while he can be lifted by the scruff of his neck where the fur is loose, there is no reason ever to do this, so don't.

Beyond the dangers already cited you may be able to think of other ones that are specific to your home— steep basement steps or the like. Go around your home and check out all potential problems—you'll be glad you did.

THE FIRST NIGHT

The first few nights a puppy spends away from his mother and littermates are quite traumatic for him. He will feel very lonely, maybe cold, and will certainly miss the heartbeat of his siblings when sleeping. To help overcome his loneliness it may help to place a clock next to his bed—one with a loud tick. This will in some way soothe him, as the clock ticks to a rhythm not dissimilar from a heart beat. A cuddly toy may also help in the first few weeks. A dim nightlight may provide some comfort to the puppy, because his eyes will not yet be fully able to see in the dark. The puppy may want to leave his bed for a drink or to relieve himself.

If the pup does whimper in the night, there are two things you should not do. One is to get up and chastise him, because he will not understand why you are shouting at him; and the other is to rush to comfort him every time he cries because he will quickly realize that if he wants you to come running all he needs to do is to holler loud enough!

These days-old pups should spend at least eight weeks with their mom and littermates before going to a new family.

By all means give your puppy some extra attention on his first night, but after this quickly refrain from so doing. The pup will cry for a while but then settle down and go to sleep. Some pups are, of course, worse than others in this respect, so you must use balanced judgment in the matter. Many owners take their pups to bed with them, and there is certainly nothing wrong with this.

The pup will be no trouble in such cases. However, you should only do this if you intend to let this be a permanent arrangement, otherwise it is hardly fair to the puppy. If you have decided to have two puppies, then they will keep each other company and you will have few problems.

Most puppies will get along with other animals. Be sure to closely supervise all introductions. Remember that animals will often come to their own understandings much more readily than we would assume.

OTHER PETS

If you have other pets in the home then the puppy must be introduced to them under careful supervision. Puppies will get on just fine with any other pets—but you must make due allowance for the respective sizes of the pets concerned, and appreciate that your puppy has a rather playful nature. It would be very foolish to leave him with a young rabbit. The pup will want to play and might bite the bunny and get altogether too rough with it. Kittens are more able to defend themselves from overly cheeky pups, who will get a quick scratch if they overstep the mark. The adult cat could obviously give the pup a very bad scratch, though generally cats will jump clear of pups and watch them from a suitable vantage point. Eventually they will meet at ground level where the cat will quickly hiss and box a puppy's ears. The pup will soon learn to respect an adult cat; thereafter they will probably develop into great friends as the pup matures into an adult dog.

HOUSETRAINING

Undoubtedly, the first form of training your puppy will undergo is in respect to his toilet habits. To achieve this you can use either newspaper, or a large litter tray filled with soil or lined with newspaper. A puppy cannot control his bowels until he is a few months old, and not fully until he is an adult. Therefore you must anticipate his needs and be prepared for a few accidents. The prime times a pup will urinate and defecate are shortly after he wakes up from a sleep, shortly after he has eaten, and after he has been playing awhile. He will usually whimper and start searching the room for a suitable place. You must quickly pick him up and place him on the newspaper or in the litter tray. Hold him in position gently but firmly. He might jump out of the box without doing anything on the first one or two occasions, but if you simply repeat the procedure every time you think he wants to relieve himself then eventually he will get the message.

When he does defecate as required, give him plenty of praise, telling him what a good puppy he is. The litter tray or newspaper must, of course, be cleaned or replaced after each use—puppies do not like using a dirty toilet any more than you do. The pup's toilet can be placed near the kitchen door and

One of the first steps toward making your puppy a welcome member of the family is getting him house trained. It is important to be patient and to keep in mind that your puppy wants to learn what you have to teach him! Jayfield's Marco and the Khan, owned by Linda Sallee-Hill.

as he gets older the tray can be placed outside while the door is open. The pup will then start to use it while he is outside. From that time on, it is easy to get the pup to use a given area of the yard.

Many breeders recommend the popular alternative of crate training. Upon bringing the pup home, introduce him to his crate. The open wire crate is the best choice, placed in a restricted, draft-free area of the home. Put the pup's Nylabone® and other favorite toys in the crate along with a wool blanket or other suitable bedding. The puppy's natural cleanliness instincts prohibit him from soiling in the place where he sleeps, his crate. The puppy should be allowed to go in and out of the open crate during the day, but he should sleep in the crate at the night and at other intervals during the day. Whenever the pup is taken out of his crate, he should be brought outside (or to his newspapers) to do his business. Never use the crate as a place of punishment. You will see how quickly your pup takes to his crate, considering it as his own safe haven from the big world around him.

Crate training is an effective way to house break your puppy. A puppy will think of his crate as his den, and no dog will mess in his living area. This fact is the basic principle of crate training.

THE EARLY DAYS

You will no doubt be given much advice on how to

bring up your puppy. This will come from dog-owning friends, neighbors, and through articles and books you may read on the subject. Some of the advice will be sound, some will be nothing short of rubbish. What you should do above all else is to keep an open mind and let common sense prevail over prejudice and worn-out ideas that have been handed down over the centuries. There is no one way that is superior to all others, no more than there is no one dog that is exactly a replica of another. Each is an individual and must always be regarded as such.

A dog never becomes disobedient, unruly, or a menace to society without the full consent of his owner. Your puppy may have many limitations, but the singular biggest limitation he is confronted with in so many instances is his owner's inability to understand his needs and how to cope with them.

Be sure to provide your puppy with some form of identification shortly after he arrives home. In the event that a puppy is lost, tags, tattooing, or microchipping will all be of great assistance in locating him.

IDENTIFICATION

It is a sad reflection on our society that the number of dogs and cats stolen every year runs into many thousands. To these can be added the number that get lost. If you do not want your cherished pet to be lost or stolen, then you should see that he is carrying a permanent identification number, as well as a temporary tag on his collar.

Permanent markings come in the form of tattoos placed either inside the pup's ear flap, or on the inner side of a pup's upper rear leg. The number given is then recorded with one of the national registration companies. Research laboratories will not purchase dogs carrying numbers as they realize these are clearly someone's pet, and not abandoned animals. As a result, thieves will normally abandon dogs so marked and this at least gives the dog a chance to be taken to the police or the dog pound, where the number can be traced and the dog reunited with its family. The only problem with this method at this time is that there are a number of registration bodies, so it is not always apparent which one the dog is registered with (as you provide the actual number). However, each registration body is aware of his competitors and will normally be happy to supply their addresses. Those holding the dog can check out which one you are with. It is not a perfect system, but until such is developed it's the best available.

Another permanent form of identification is the microchip, a computer chip that is no bigger than a grain of rice, that is injected between the dog's shoulder blades. The dog feels no discomfort. The dog also receives a tag that says he is microchipped. If the dog is lost and picked up by the humane society, they can trace the owner by scanning the microchip. It is the safest form of identification.

A temporary tag takes the form of a metal or plastic disk large enough for you to place the dog's name and your phone number on it—maybe even your address as well. In virtually all places you will be required to obtain a license for your puppy. This may not become applicable until the pup is six months old, but it might apply regardless of his age. Much depends upon the state within a country, or the country itself, so check with your veterinarian if the breeder has not already advised you on this.

GROOMING YOUR SMOOTH FOX TERRIER

The Smooth Fox Terrier does not require a lot of grooming. His short coat makes for easy maintenance. Simply brush him, clip his nails and keep his pads clean.

Although, in terms of grooming, the Smooth Fox Terrier is basically a low-maintenance dog, there is definitely some tidying up to be done on a Smooth for the show ring. Hair grows equally over the entire body and to give the clean, smooth outline desired, certain

Getting your Smooth used to grooming at an early age is recommended. It will be easier for all concerned if your Smooth knows what to expect. You never know—he may grow to enjoy the attention!

areas must be scissored or clippered. For pet mainte-nance, brushing the coat, keeping the nails trimmed, and cleaning the hair out of the pads of the feet is sufficient.

Should you decide to keep your Smooth looking spiffy, all you need is a pair of electric clippers, a comb, a brush, and some time. With the clippers, clean the underside of the throat and sides of the neck—always clipping in the direction of the hair growth. Carefully smooth off the back of the tail, and clean out the belly, if needed. With thinning scissors, blend the coat on the sides of the ridge of the neck so there is no telltale line. You may need to do some blending into the shoulders, and the tail. With regular shears, cleanly cut the hair from the "tuck-up" area. On the rump or cheeks, scissor "buns," i.e.; you will need to trim fairly closely on either side of the anus, but leave the coat a bit longer about an inch to two inches down. Even up all scraggly hair in the turn of the stifle, the lower chest must be shaped and trimmed, and neaten the feet and legs. Look at the head and if your dog is a bit wide, some deft thinning on the cheeks may make a prettier picture. Neaten the ears of long hair, cut the whiskers, give him a bath, and he is as presentable as any show dog!

FEEDING YOUR SMOOTH FOX TERRIER

Today there are literally hundreds of prepared foods on the market for your dog. Many are specially formulated for puppies. Be sure to ask your breeder for some general guidelines as to what and how much your pup should be eating.

Dog owners today are fortunate in that they live in an age when considerable cash has been invested in the study of canine nutritional requirements. This means dog food manufacturers are very concerned about ensuring that their foods are of the best quality. The result of all of their studies, apart from the food itself, is that dog owners are bombarded with advertisements telling them why they must purchase a given brand. The number of products available to you is unlimited, so it is hardly surprising to find that dogs in general suffer from obesity and an excess of vitamins, rather than the reverse. Be sure to feed age-appropriate food—puppy food up to one year of age, adult food thereafter. Generally breeders recommend dry food supplemented by canned, if needed.

FACTORS AFFECTING NUTRITIONAL NEEDS

Activity Level. A dog that lives in a country environment and is able to exercise for long periods of the day will need more food than the same breed of dog living in an apartment and given little exercise.

Quality of the Food. Obviously the quality of food will affect the quantity required by a puppy. If the nutritional content of a food is low then the puppy will need more of it than if a better quality food was fed.

Balance of Nutrients and Vitamins. Feeding a puppy the correct balance of nutrients is not easy because the average person is not able to measure out ratios of one to another, so it is a case of trying to see that nothing is in excess. However, only tests, or your veterinarian, can be the source of reliable advice.

Genetic and Biological Variation. Apart from all of the other considerations, it should be remembered that each puppy is an individual. His genetic make-up will influence not only his physical characteristics but also his metabolic efficiency. This being so, two pups from the same litter can vary quite a bit in the amount of food they need to perform the

Activity level is one of the determining factors when deciding what type of food to offer your dog. There are different formulations now available to correspond to a dog's many needs.

same function under the same conditions. If you consider the potential combinations of all of these factors then you will see that pups of a given breed could vary quite a bit in the amount of food they will need. Before discussing feeding quantities it is valuable to know at least a little about the composition of food and its role in the body.

COMPOSITION AND ROLE OF FOOD

The main ingredients of food are protein, fats, and carbohydrates, each of which is needed in relatively large quantities when compared to the other needs of vitamins and minerals. The other vital ingredient of food is, of course, water. Although all foods obviously contain some of the basic ingredients needed for an animal to survive, they do not all contain the ingredients in the needed ratios or type. For example, there are many forms of protein, just as there are many types of carbohydrates. Both of these compounds are found in meat and in vegetable matter—but not all of those that are needed will be in one particular meat or vegetable. Plants, especially, do not contain certain amino acids that are required for the synthesis of certain proteins needed by dogs.

Likewise, vitamins are found in meats and vegetable matter, but vegetables are a richer source of most. Meat contains very little carbohydrates. Some vitamins can be synthesized by the dog, so do not need to be supplied via the food. Dogs are carnivores and this means their digestive tract has evolved to need a high quantity of meat as com-

Carrots are rich in fiber, carbohydrates and vitamin A. The Carrot Bone™ from Nylabone® is a durable chew containing no plastics or artificial ingredients of any kind. It can be served as-is, in a bone-hard form, or microwaved to a biscuit consistency—whichever your Smooth prefers.

pared to humans. The digestive system of carnivores is unable to break down the tough cellulose walls of plant matter, but it is easily able to assimilate proteins from meat.

In order to gain its needed vegetable matter in a form that it can cope with, the carnivore eats all of its prey. This includes the partly digested food within the stomach. In commercially prepared foods, the cellulose is broken down by cooking. During this process the vitamin content is either greatly reduced or lost altogether. The manufacturer therefore adds vitamins once the heat process has been completed. This is why commercial foods are so useful as part of a feeding regimen, providing they are of good quality and from a company that has prepared the foods very carefully.

Your Smooth will be happier and his teeth and gums healthier if you give him a POPpup™ to chew on. Every POPpup™ is 100% edible and enhanced with dog friendly ingredients like liver, cheese, spinach, chicken, carrots, or potatoes. What you won't find in a POPpup™ is salt, sugar, alcohol, plastic, or preservatives. You can even microwave a POPpup™ to turn it into a huge crackly treat for your Smooth to enjoy.

Proteins

These are made from amino acids, of which at least ten are essential if a puppy is to maintain healthy growth. Proteins provide the building blocks for the puppy's body. The richest sources are meat, fish and poultry, together with their by-products. The latter will include milk, cheese, yogurt, fishmeal, and eggs. Vegetable matter that has a high protein content includes soy beans, together with numerous corn and other plant extracts that have been dehydrated. The actual protein content needed in the diet will be determined both by the activity level of the dog and his age. The total protein need will also be influenced by the digestibility factor of the food given.

Fats

These serve numerous roles in the puppy's body. They provide insulation against the cold, and help buffer the organs from knocks and general activity shocks. They provide the richest source of energy, and reserves of this, and they are vital in the transport of vitamins and other nutrients, via the blood, to all other organs. Finally, it is the fat content within a diet that gives it palatability. It is important that the fat content of a diet should not be excessive. This is because the high energy content of fats (more than twice that of protein or carbohydrate) will increase the overall energy content of the diet. The puppy will adjust its food intake to that of its energy needs, which are obviously more easily met in a high-energy diet. This will mean that while the fats are providing the energy needs of the puppy, the over-all diet may not be providing its protein, vitamin, and mineral needs, so signs of protein deficiency will become apparent. Rich sources of fats are meat, their byproducts (butter, milk), and vegetable oils, such as safflower, olive, corn or soy bean.

To combat boredom and relieve your Smooth's natural desire to chew, there's nothing better than a Roar-Hide™. Unlike common rawhide, this bone won't turn into a gooey mess when chewed on, so your dog won't choke on small pieces of it, and your carpet won't be stained by it. The Roar-Hide™ is completely edible and is high in protein (over 86%) and low in fat (less than 1/3 of 1%). The Roar-Hide™ is just right for your Smooth.

Carbohydrates

These are the principal energy compounds given to puppies and adult dogs. Their inclusion within most commercial brand dog foods is for cost, rather than dietary needs. These compounds are more commonly known as sugars, and they are seen in simple or complex compounds of carbon, hydrogen, and oxygen. One of the simple sugars is called glucose, and it is vital

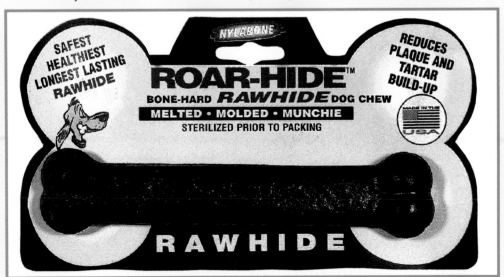

to many metabolic processes. When large chains of glucose are created, they form compound sugars. One of these is called glycogen, and it is found in the cells of animals. Another, called starch, is the material that is found in the cells of plants.

Vitamins

These are not foods as such but chemical compounds that assist in all aspects of an animal's life. They help in so many ways that to attempt to describe these effectively would require a chapter in itself. Fruits are a rich source of vitamins, as is the liver of most animals. Many vitamins are unstable and easily destroyed by light, heat, moisture, or rancidity. An excess of vitamins, especially A and D, has been proven to be very harmful. Provided a puppy is receiving a balanced diet, it is most unlikely there will be a deficiency, whereas hypervitaminosis (an excess of vitamins) has become quite common due to owners and breeders feeding unneeded supplements. The only time you should feed extra vitamins to your puppy is if your veterinarian advises you to.

Minerals

These provide strength to bone and cell tissue, as well as assist in many metabolic processes. Examples are calcium, phosphorous, copper, iron, magnesium, selenium, potassium, zinc, and sodium. The recommended amounts of all minerals in the diet has not been fully established. Calcium and phosphorous are known to be important, especially to puppies. They help in forming strong bone. As with vitamins, a mineral deficiency is most unlikely in pups given a good and varied diet. Again, an excess can create problems—this applying equally to calcium.

Water

This is the most important of all nutrients, as is easily shown by the fact that the adult dog is made up of about 60 percent water, the puppy containing an even higher percentage. Dogs must retain a water balance, which means that the total intake should be balanced by the total output. The intake comes either by direct input (the tap or its equivalent), plus water released when food is oxidized, known as metabolic water (remember that all foods contain the elements hydrogen and oxygen that

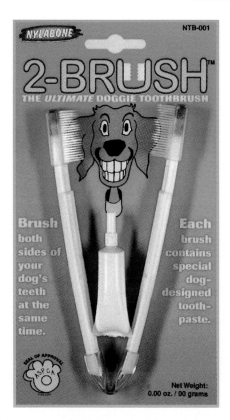

2-Brush™ by Nylabone® is made with two toothbrushes to clean both sides of your dog's teeth at the same time. Each brush contains a reservoir designed to apply the toothpaste, which is specially formulated for dogs, directly into the toothbrush.

recombine in the body to create water). A dog without adequate water will lose condition more rapidly than one depleted of food, a fact common to most animal species.

AMOUNT TO FEED

The best way to determine dietary requirements is by observing the puppy's general health and physical appearance. If he is well covered with flesh, shows good bone development and muscle, and is an active alert puppy, then his diet is fine. A puppy will consume about twice as much as an adult (of the same breed). You should ask the breeder of your puppy to show you the amounts fed to their pups and this will be a good starting point.

The puppy should eat his meal in about five to seven minutes. Any leftover food can be discarded or placed into the refrigerator until the next meal (but be sure it is thawed fully if your fridge is very cold).

If the puppy quickly devours its meal and is clearly still hungry, then you are not giving him enough food. If he eats readily but then begins to pick at it, or walks away leaving a quantity, then you are probably giving him too much food. Adjust this at the next meal and you will quickly begin to appreciate what the correct amount is. If, over a number of weeks, the pup starts to look fat, then he is obviously overeating; the reverse is true if he starts to look thin compared with others of the same breed.

WHEN TO FEED

It really does not matter what times of the day the puppy is fed, as long as he receives the needed quantity of food. Puppies from 8 weeks to 12 or 16 weeks need 3 or 4 meals a day. Older puppies and adult dogs should be fed twice a day. What is most important is that the feeding times are reasonably regular. They can be tailored to fit in with your own timetable—for example, 7 a.m. and 6 p.m. The dog will then expect his meals at these times each day. Keeping regular feeding times and feeding set amounts will help you monitor your puppy's or dog's health. If a dog that's normally enthusiastic about mealtimes and eats readily suddenly shows a lack of interest in food, you'll know something's not right.

It really does not matter when a puppy is fed as long as he is receiving the correct quantity of food. However, once a pup has become used to set meal times he will expect you to be most punctual!

TRAINING YOUR SMOOTH FOX TERRIER

Once your puppy has settled into his new home and responds to his name you can begin his training.

Once your puppy has settled into your home and responds to his name, then you can begin his basic training. Before giving advice on how you should go about doing this, two important points should be made. You should train the puppy in isolation of any potential distractions, and you should keep all lessons very short. It is essential that you have the full attention of your puppy. This is not possible if there are other people about, or televisions and radios on, or other pets in the vicinity. Even when the pup has become a young adult, the maximum time you should allocate to a lesson is about 20 minutes. However, you can give the puppy more than one lesson a day, three being as many as are recommended, each well spaced apart.

Before beginning a lesson, always play a little game with the puppy so he is in an active state of mind and thus more receptive to the matter at hand. Likewise, always end a lesson with fun-time for the pup, and always—this is most important—end on a high note, praising the puppy. Let the lesson end when the pup has done as you require so he receives lots of fuss. This will really build his confidence.

Training a puppy to his collar and leash is not difficult. Most puppies will simply forget anything is different after a few moments wearing a collar. After dragging a leash behind him for a bit, that too will lose its novelty.

COLLAR AND LEASH TRAINING

Training a puppy to his collar and leash is very easy. Place a collar on the puppy and, although he will initially try to bite at it, he will soon forget it, the more so if you play with him. You can leave the collar on for a few hours. Some people leave their dogs' collars on all of the time, others only when they are taking the dog out. If it is to be left on, purchase a narrow or round one so it does not mark the fur.

Once the puppy ignores his collar, then you can attach the leash to it and let the puppy pull this along behind it for a few minutes. However, if the pup starts to chew at the leash, simply hold the leash but keep it slack and let the pup go where he wants. The idea is to let him get the feel of the leash, but not get in the habit of chewing it. Repeat this a couple of times a day for two days and the pup will get used to the leash without thinking that it will restrain him—which you will not have attempted to do yet.

Be sure to begin your puppy's training sessions away from the distractions of other people and animals. Also, keep your lessons short—no more than 20 minutes at a time—your pup shouldn't be expected to concentrate for longer than that.

Next, you can let the pup understand that the leash will restrict his movements. The first time he realizes this, he will pull and buck or just sit down. Immediately call the pup to you and give him lots of fuss. Never tug on the leash so the puppy is dragged along the floor, as this simply implants a negative thought in his mind.

THE COME COMMAND

Come is the most vital of all commands and especially so for the independently minded dog. To teach the puppy to come, let him reach the end of a long lead, then give the command and his name, gently pulling him toward you at the same time. As soon as he associates the word come with the action of moving toward you, pull only when he does not respond immediately. As he starts to come, move back to make him learn that he must come from a distance as well as when he is close to you. Soon you may be able to practice without a leash, but if he is slow to come or notably disobedient, go to him and pull him toward you, repeating the command. Never scold a dog during this exercise—or any other exercise. Remember the trick is that the puppy must want to come to you. For the very independent dog, hand signals may work better than verbal commands.

Come is one of the most important commands, and is essential to all other lessons. It can be taught verbally or with hand signals.

THE SIT COMMAND

As with most basic commands, your puppy will learn this one in just a few lessons. You can give the puppy two lessons a day on the sit command but he will make just as much progress with one 15-minute lesson each day. Some trainers will advise you that you should not proceed to other commands until the previous one has been learned really well. However,

A bright young pup can handle more than one command a lesson. Remember it is important to begin and end each lesson on a high note, having successfully completed something.

a bright young pup is quite capable of handling more than one command per lesson, and certainly per day. Indeed, as time progresses, you will be going through each command as a matter of routine before a new one is attempted. This is so the puppy always starts, as well as ends, a lesson on a high note, having successfully completed something.

Call the puppy to you and fuss over him. Place one hand on his hindquarters and the other under his upper chest. Say "Sit" in a pleasant (never harsh) voice. At the same time, push down his rear end and push up under his chest. Now lavish praise on the puppy. Repeat this a few times and your pet will get the idea. Once the puppy is in the sit position you will release your hands. At first he will tend to get up, so immediately repeat the exercise. The lesson will end when the pup is in the sit position. When the puppy understands the command, and does it right away, you can slowly move backwards so that you are a few feet away from him. If he attempts to come to you, simply place him back in the original position and start again. Do not attempt to keep the pup in the sit position for too long. At this age, even a few seconds is a long while and you do not want him to get bored with lessons before he has even begun them.

Once your puppy has mastered the sit command you can begin taking lovely pictures like this one. The fact is, training will make your dog happy, and his life more fulfilling. A well-trained dog will be able to accompany you almost anywhere and participate in all aspects of your life.

THE HEEL COMMAND

All dogs should be able to walk nicely on a leash without their owners being involved in a tug-of-war. The heel command will follow leash training. Heel training is best done where you have a wall to one side of you. This will restrict the puppy's lateral movements, so you only have to contend with forward and

All dogs should be able to walk on a leash nicely, however the heel command is especially important in the show ring.

backward situations. A fence is an alternative, or you can do the lesson in the garage. Again, it is better to do the lesson in private, not on a public sidewalk where there will be many distractions.

With a puppy, there will be no need to use a choke collar as you can be just as effective with a regular one. The leash should be of good length, certainly not too short. You can adjust the space between you, the puppy, and the wall so your pet has only a small amount of room to move sideways. This being so, he will either hang back or pull ahead—the latter is the more desirable state as it indicates a bold pup who is not frightened of you.

Hold the leash in your right hand and pass it through your left. As the puppy moves ahead and strains on the leash, give the leash a quick jerk backwards with your left hand, at the same time saying "Heel." The position you want the pup to be in is such that his chest is level with, or just behind, an imaginary line from your knee. When the puppy is in this position, praise him and begin walking again, and the whole exercise will be repeated. Once the puppy begins to get the message, you can use your left hand to pat the side of your knee so the pup is encouraged to keep close to your side.

It is useful to suddenly do an about-turn when the pup understands the basics. The puppy will now be behind you, so you can pat your knee and say "Heel." As soon as the pup is in the correct position, give him lots of praise. The puppy will now be beginning to associate certain words with certain actions. When-

Once a dog understands the heel command it will make walking him in public places a much more pleasurable experience. Your dog will stay close to your side instead of straining to engage everyone you pass.

ever he is not in the heel position he will experience displeasure as you jerk the leash, but when he comes alongside you he will receive praise. Given these two options, he will always prefer the latter—assuming he has no other reason to fear you, which would then create a dilemma in his mind.

Remember one of the most important aspects of training is praise. Your dog will always want to do what pleases you. When he responds to a command correctly praise him lavishly, if correction is needed be sure you are not too harsh.

Once the lesson has been well learned, then you can adjust your pace from a slow walk to a quick one and the puppy will come to adjust. The slow walk is always the more difficult for most puppies, as they are usually anxious to be on the move.

If you have no wall to walk against then things will be a little more difficult because the pup will tend to wander to his left. This means you need to give lateral jerks as well as bring the pup to your side. End the lesson when the pup is walking nicely beside you.

Begin the lesson with a few sit commands (which he understands by now), so you're starting with success and praise. If your puppy is nervous on the leash, you should never drag him to your side as you may see so many other people do (who obviously didn't invest in a good book like you did!). If the pup sits down, call him to your side and give lots of praise. The pup must always come to you because he wants to. If he is dragged to your side he will see you doing the drag-ging—a big negative. When he races ahead he does not see you jerk the leash, so all he knows is that something restricted his movement and, once he was in a given position, you gave him lots of praise. This is using canine psychology to your advantage.

Always try to remember that if a dog must be disciplined, then try not to let him associate the discipline with you. This is not possible in all matters but, where it is, this is definitely to be preferred.

THE STAY COMMAND

This command follows from the sit. Face the puppy and say "Sit." Now step backwards, and as you do, say "Stay." Let the pup remain in the position for only a few seconds before calling him to you and giving lots of praise. Repeat this, but step further back. You do not need to shout at the puppy. Your pet is not deaf; in fact, his hearing is far better than yours. Speak just loudly enough for the pup to hear, yet use a firm voice. You can stretch the word to form a "sta-a-a-y." If the pup gets up and comes to you simply lift him up, place him back in the original position, and start again. As the pup comes to understand the command, you can move further and further back.

The next test is to walk away after placing the pup. This will mean your back is to him, which will tempt him to follow you. Keep an eye over your shoulder, and the minute the pup starts to move, spin around and, using a sterner voice, say either "Sit" or "Stay." If the pup has gotten quite close to you, then, again, return him to the original position.

As the weeks go by you can increase the length of time the pup is left in the stay position—but two to three minutes is quite long enough for a puppy. If your puppy drops into a lying position and is clearly more comfortable, there is nothing wrong with this. Like-wise, your pup will want to face the direction in which you walked off. Some trainers will insist that the dog faces the direction he was placed in, regardless of

The stay command will allow you to leave your puppy's side knowing that he will stay where you put him. At first you will only be several feet from your pup, but as training continues you will be able to increase distance and sometimes move out of your puppy's sight entirely.

whether you move off on his blind side. I have never believed in this sort of obedience because it has no practical benefit.

THE DOWN COMMAND

From the puppy's viewpoint, the down command can be one of the more difficult ones to accept. This is because the position is one taken up by a submissive dog in a wild pack situation. A timid dog will roll over—a natural gesture of submission. A bolder pup will want to get up, and might back off, not feeling he should have to submit to this command. He will feel that he is under attack from you and about to be punished—which is what would be the position in his natural environment. Once he comes to understand this is not the case, he will accept this unnatural position without any problem.

You may notice that some dogs will sit very quickly, but will respond to the down command more slowly—it is their way of saying that they will obey the command, but under protest!

There are two ways to teach this command. One is, in my mind, more intimidating than the other, but it is up to you to decide which one works best for you. The first method is to stand in front of your puppy and bring him to the sit position, with his collar and leash on. Pass the leash under your left foot so that when you pull on it, the result is that the pup's neck is forced downwards. With your free left hand, push the pup's shoulders down while at the same time saying "Down." This is when a bold pup will instantly try to back off and wriggle in full protest. Hold the pup firmly by the shoulders so he stays in the position for a second or two, then tell him what a good dog he is and give him lots of praise. Repeat this only a few times in a lesson because otherwise the puppy will get bored and upset over this command. End with an easy command that brings back the pup's confidence.

The second method, and the one I prefer, is done as follows: Stand in front of the pup and then tell him to sit. Now kneel down, which is immediately far less intimidating to the puppy than to have you towering above him. Take each of his front legs and pull them forward, at the same time saying "Down." Release the legs and quickly apply light pressure on the shoulders with your left hand. Then, as quickly, say "Good boy"

The down command can be the most difficult for a puppy to accept. In the wild the down command represents the position of a submissive dog, as soon as he realizes this isn't the case, your pup should have no further problems.

and give lots of fuss. Repeat two or three times only. The pup will learn over a few lessons. Remember, this is a very submissive act on the pup's behalf, so there is no need to rush matters.

RECALL TO HEEL COMMAND

When your puppy is coming to the heel position from an off-leash situation—such as if he has been running free—he should do this in the correct manner. He should pass behind you and take up his position and then sit. To teach this command, have the pup in front of you in the sit position with his collar and leash on. Hold the leash in your right hand. Give him the command to heel, and pat your left knee. As the pup starts to move forward, use your right hand to guide him behind you. If need be you can hold his collar and walk the dog around the back of you to the desired position. You will need to repeat this a few times until the dog understands what is wanted.

When he has done this a number of times, you can try it without the collar and leash. If the pup comes up toward your left side, then bring him to the sit position in front of you, hold his collar and walk him around the back of you. He will eventually understand and automatically pass around your back each time. If the dog is already behind you when you recall him, then he should automatically come to your left side, which you will be patting with your hand.

When your puppy is coming to the heel position from an off leash situation he must pass behind you, take up his position and then sit. The recall to heel command is very helpful when training a dog for the field or just letting him have a run in the park.

THE NO COMMAND

This is a command that must be obeyed every time without fail. There are no halfway stages, he must be 100-percent reliable. Most delinquent dogs have never been taught this command; included in these are the jumpers, the barkers, and the biters. Were your puppy to approach a poisonous snake or any other potential danger, the no command, coupled with the recall, could save his life. You do not need to give a specific lesson for this command because it will crop up time and again in day-to-day life.

If the puppy is chewing a slipper, you should approach the pup, take hold of the slipper, and say "No" in a stern voice. If he jumps onto the furniture, lift him off and say "No" and place him gently on the floor. You must be consistent in the use of the command and apply it every time he is doing something you do not want him to do.

Opposite: Whether your Smooth Fox Terrier becomes a show dog, service dog, participates in obedience or agility trials, or is a companion dog, he should always be the champion of your heart! Raybills Bittersweet, owned by Jerry Moon and Hans Rietz.

Opportunities to teach the no command will present themselves daily. Whenever your pup does something he shouldn't be doing correct him with a firm "No." This is a command that must be obeyed every time it is given without fail.

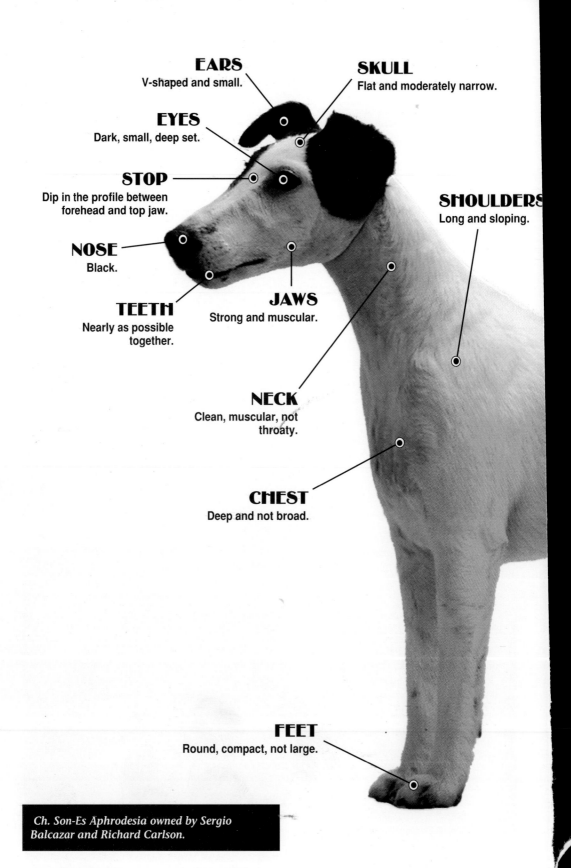

EARS
V-shaped and small.

SKULL
Flat and moderately narrow.

EYES
Dark, small, deep set.

STOP
Dip in the profile between forehead and top jaw.

SHOULDERS
Long and sloping.

NOSE
Black.

TEETH
Nearly as possible together.

JAWS
Strong and muscular.

NECK
Clean, muscular, not throaty.

CHEST
Deep and not broad.

FEET
Round, compact, not large.

Ch. Son-Es Aphrodesia owned by Sergio Balcazar and Richard Carlson.